# HOW TO DEFEAT SATAN'S NUMBER 1 WEAPON

Keith A. Craft

How to Defeat Satan's Number 1 Weapon

COPYRIGHT © 1996 by Keith A. Craft

Unless otherwise noted, all scriptures are from the Holy Bible, New International Version, Copyright ©1973, 1984, International Bible Society. Used by permission of Zondervan Bible Publishers

Scriptures marked KJV are from the King James Version

This book, or parts thereof, may not be reproduced in any form without permission from the publisher. Exceptions are made for brief excerpts in published reviews.

Published by

1% Publishing
8500 Teel Parkway
Frisco, Texas 75034

ISBN 978-1-7330945-3-5

Printed in the United States of America

# CONTENTS

|   | Introduction | 7 |
|---|---|---|
| 1 | The Secret Mission | 11 |
| 2 | Living on Purpose | 21 |
| 3 | Cancer of the Spirit | 33 |
| 4 | Where Does it Begin? | 45 |
| 5 | The Revealing Results | 55 |
| 6 | Truth or Consequences? | 67 |
| 7 | Breaking the Addiction | 77 |
| 8 | The Cure | 87 |

## *Dedication*

This book is dedicated to my hero — my "Mammaw."

She is the one person who has always believed in me. Since the day of my birth there has been a special bond between us. As an infant, after suffocating in a plastic bag, she prayed me back to life and has continued to pray for me every day. She is an indomitable example of what a Christian really is.

If there was ever an individual who had the right to be negative, it would be Mammaw. After raising four children, her husband walked out on her. She was diagnosed with breast cancer and had a radical mastectomy. The radiation that was used to treat her burned and scarred the left side of her body so severely that she has suffered on-going chronic physical problems for more than thirty-five years. Recently it was discovered that during all of this time she has had only forty percent usage of one lung.

My Mammaw, my hero. Cancer could not kill her, divorce could not destroy her, and physical suffering has not soured her. Like Paul, she can truly say, "I have finished my course, I have kept the faith: Henceforth there is laid up for me a crown of righteousness which the Lord, the righteous judge, shall give me at that last day" (2 Timothy 4:7-8)

She is the fabric that gives strength to this message.

Thank you Mammaw, for being my inspiration.

# INTRODUCTION

All my life I have heard how Satan is a crafty, cunning deceiver whose aim is to destroy the faith of believers and keep sinners in his grasp.

Then one day, as I was reading one of the most overlooked stories in the Old Testament, I realized that the devil has a secret weapon ready to use against us. In fact, it is his number one weapon.

Aaron and Miriam, the brother and sister of Moses, fell prey to the ultimate scheme of Satan. Their works and actions not only unleashed a horrible spirit in the camp of the children of Israel, but brought the wrath of the Almighty.

What was the result of this "cancer of the spirit"? It produced almost total defeat in the desert and the same plot is being used to this very day.

Yes, the devil has specific plans and you need to be totally aware of what they are. Even more, he has a weapon designed to keep you from having a right relationship with God. His objective is to strike at the very purpose of your life.

In my travels across America and in foreign nations, I meet people every day who have fallen into Satan's snare. Almost without knowing it, they have been attacked at their weakest point---and are being destroyed from the inside out.

The message of this book is one that is rarely heard from pulpits, seldom written about, almost never discussed, yet its consequences affect nearly every aspect of your life.

The secret scheme Satan has against you is about to be exposed. Not only will you be aware of his evil intentions and deceitful plans, you will also learn how to break the powerful addiction he inflicts on you.

In the process, you will win a personal battle against the evil one and be able to help those who may be trapped in the same web.

On the pages that follow, you'll find answers to these questions:

- What are Satan's secret plans of attack?
- How can I recognize the devil's diversions?
- How can seeds of rebellion be turned into seeds of righteousness?
- How can roots of jealousy be exchanged for joy and blessing?

- What are the great mistakes Christians make, and how can they be avoided?
- What are the short and long term consequences of the devil's scheme and what action should I take?
- What are the vital steps that produce purpose, peace and prosperity?

I pray this book will not only be a revelation of what the devil has planned but will equip you to totally defeat Satan's number one weapon.

---

Special thanks to Pastor David Long and the congregation of Believers Life Assembly in Harvey, Louisiana, for helping make this book possible.

— Keith A. Craft

## CHAPTER 1

# THE SECRET MISSION

*I believe Satan to exist for two reasons:
First, the Bible says so; and second,
I've done business with him.*
– Dwight L. Moody

Let's stop kidding ourselves. We may think we have got it made---driving a new car, wearing fashionable clothes, and making great plans for the future. Lurking in the shadows, however, is an invisible enemy that has you in the cross hairs of his rifle. He is in position, ready to pull the trigger.

Here is what Jesus has to say about the purpose of your soul's greatest adversary: "The thief cometh not, but for to steal, and to kill, and to destroy" (John 10:10 KJV).

Who was He talking about? Satan—the prince of darkness.

Fortunately, there is more to the message Christ delivered. The next word in the verse has only one letter, but it is as important as any in Scripture. It is a gigantic "I." Jesus completed His declaration with this significant statement: " I am come that they might have life and that they might have it more abundantly" (v.10).

## Why Was He Sent?

During the past few years I've asked this question many times: "Why do you believe God sent His Son to earth?" The answers most people give are true, but they are incomplete.

**First: God did not send Jesus to earth only to die on the Cross for our sins---although I'm glad He did.**

The axis on which the Gospel pivots is found in these words: "For God so loved the world, that he gave his only begotten Son, that whosoever believeth in him should not perish, but have everlasting life" (John 3:16 KJV)

From Genesis to Revelation if there was no John 3:16, there would be no purpose for God's message for man.

**Second: God did not send Jesus to the cross only to die for our healing—yet again, I'm thankful He did.**

In 1977, when I was seventeen, we were in a great church in New Orleans that had five services on Sunday Morning, with nearly two thousand people in each meeting. I was in the third service and, unknown to the pastor, I was suffering because I had broken the big toe on my left foot.

As a high school basketball player on a team that was about to enter the district playoffs, having a broken toe was devastating.

Suddenly, in the middle of the service, the pastor stopped and declared, "Somebody here has a broken left big toe."

Miraculously, God healed me. I became a testimony to my high school team about the Lord's healing power.

What God revealed to the prophet Isaiah about the coming Messiah was true. "He was wounded for our transgressions, he was bruised for our iniquities: the chastisement of our peace was upon him; and with his stripes we are healed" (Isaiah 53:5 KJV)

Yes, God sent Jesus to die for our sins and our sickness; however, there are many people who do not understand the true significance of the Cross.

**THE ULTIMATE REASON JESUS DIED ON THE CROSS WAS TO GIVE US FREEDOM FROM SATAN.**

I have grown up in church. As a "bonafide" church boy, I have observed many people who are born again and Spirit-filled, but not free. In other words, they are regenerated, but not liberated.

Scripture reveals, "For this purpose the Son of God was manifest, that he might destroy the works of the devil" (1 John 3:8 KJV)

## The Enemy's Plans

Is Satan plotting against you? Yes! Is the devil designing a strategy to trap you? Absolutely! That's exactly what he's scheming and thinking about every second.

Later in this book we will expose Satan's number one weapon against you. First, let's look at the devil's two biggest plans.

**Satan's Plan Number One:** *To keep you from entering into a right relationship with God.*

The devil has already written his obituary for your life. It's called failure.

- He wants you to fail in your marriage.
- He wants you to fail in your business.
- He wants you to fail in your health, your finances and in your alliance with the Almighty.

Nothing would please the adversary more than enticing you to settle for what is simply "good" or average. Years ago I heard a phrase that I continually think about:

*Never allow the good to become*
*robber of the best.*

Why did Jesus come to destroy the works of Satan?

God knows Satan. He knows that the devil has a plan to steal, kill and destroy. The devil's goal is to keep you from knowing God, but Christ came to give you freedom.

- Freedom from all the encumbrances of sin.
- Freedom to walk by faith and not by sight.
- Freedom from other people's opinion.
- Freedom to be all God has created you to be.
- Freedom from the traditions of man.
- Freedom to enter into a right relationship with God.

Many Christians do not realize the devil accepts the fact that you are going to spend eternity in heaven. However, his plan for you is to get you focused on situations, circumstances and relational difficulties to rob you of your joy. If you have no joy or evidence in your life of God's freedom, Satan knows he has rendered you ineffective for the kingdom of God. He knows you are going to heaven, but his demonic delusion is for no one else to know----and thereby cause your influence for Christ to be of no effect.

**Satan's Plan Number Two:** *To keep you focused on what is temporary rather than what is eternal.*

The devil must readily accept the loss of your soul when you are born again.

If he can't keep your from having a right relationship with God, I can guarantee you that Satan will muster everything in his power to make you as miserable as possible this side of eternity.

What happens if Lucifer fails at his first objective? Plan Number Two automatically kicks in. He will constantly attempt to shift your focus to things that really don't matter. He'd love nothing more than for you to waste your time making huge mountains out of tiny molehills.

The devil's blueprint includes beguiling you to be governed by the seen realm rather than the unseen realm.

Remember, the power of the Cross is not only that our sins are forgiven and our bodies are made whole, but that we are free from earthly limitations and physical restrictions. He made it possible for us to move into the realm of the Spirit. Through Christ we can have liberty from being governed by circumstances or relational difficulties. We can be free to become everything God created us to be.

It is faith that makes it possible for our focus to be on things eternal.

## Reformed or Deformed?

In our travels across America I encounter Christians who seem to be spiritually deformed. To be deformed means to "be put out of shape."

The enemy knows what to use to "deform" us. He knows that God wants us to be "reformed," which means "to be made better by the removal of errors."

I have discovered that martial arts and Christianity have some things in common. In the initial stage of martial arts training, you are taught "forms." The purpose of the form is to teach discipline and coordination. Once you know the motions by heart, you can effectively defend yourself.

Next, you are taught to add some sound to help generate maximum force and energy from the inside out. When you've got the pattern down to a science, you begin to express yourself within the form. The sounds expressed become an outward manifestation of the power you feel on the inside.

The problem with martial arts is the false sense of confidence it can bring. You can have all the forms down. You shout loudly with expression, but if you are being robbed at gunpoint, it will do you no good. Why? Because all of your knowledge and skill of martial arts cannot stop a bullet.

> *When we come to Christ, He wants to reform us---not after the traditions of man, but after the Spirit of God.*

Jesus wants to bring correction into our lives, so we can have continual direction and live victoriously.

While God wants us reformed, the devil wants us deformed. We become deformed spiritually when we are governed by what is in the seen realm, rather than walking by faith.

Sadly, many people who claim to be free in Christ, sing praises to God on Sunday, but speak curses about the boss of other people, fight with their spouse, and lose their temper with those who they don't agree with.

The apostle Paul warns us about people "having a form of godliness, but denying its power" (2 Timothy 3:5)

## The Roaring Lion

Satan is carefully watching. "Be sober, be vigilant; because your adversary, the devil, as a roaring lion, walketh about, seeking whom he may devour"! (Peter 5:8 KJV)

He says to himself, "They know the forms, they have learned the songs, but I know what I can use against them. I have the bullet that can penetrate their outward form." He says, "I'll divert their attention to people and embroil their emotions in personal conflicts.

> *The devil doesn't care if you sing, shout, quote the Psalms or dance in the Spirit as long as he knows he can quickly shift your focus to things that have no eternal value.*

Satan is not concerned with your confession, he only wants to rob you of your confidence and joy. Never forget that his ultimate mission and objective is to steal, kill and destroy.

By causing you to concentrate on what is happening in your life, you are looking around you instead of above. You're engrossed in earthly happenings instead of seeking answers from heaven.

Pause for a moment to answer this question. What is currently the primary focus of your life?

- Is it the stress of your job?
- Is it financial pressure?
- Is it anxiety about your health?
- Is it a strained relationship?

Those are Satan's diversionary bullets. Your principle objective---above all else—is to have a divine relationship with God.

You may have been raised in the best home, never smoked, used alcohol or drugs, or engaged in immorality, but never forget that Satan has a plan against you.

Every time you center on the temporary rather than the eternal, he is winning the struggle for your soul.

Long ago, Thomas á Kempis declared, "The devil never sleeps, and your flesh is very much alive. Prepare yourself for battle. Surrounding you are enemies that never rest."

Get ready to wage war. Get ready to overcome the devil's number one secret weapon against you. Next, we will expose his attacks against you.

CHAPTER 2

# LIVING ON PURPOSE

*All men should strive to learn before they
die
What they are running from,
and to, and why.*
— James Thurber

When I was in the eighth grade, our family attended a small but exciting church in Grand Prairie, Texas.

One Sunday morning the pastor stopped in the middle of his message and said, "I want everyone to look at your hands."

Then he made a simple statement that has had a profound impact on my life. He declared, "God made your hands just the way they are—for His purpose."

At 14 years of age, I wore a size 14 shoe. I was a skinny teenager with pimples to prove it. Like many young people, I was struggling with my own significance and self-confidence.

That morning the Lord reminded me that I had been reformed for a reason. As I looked at my hands, I felt a sense of destiny. For the first time in my life, I became consciously aware of the fact that God had a purpose for my life.

## Blatant Attacks

Satan has a diabolical strategy—specific plans as we have discussed, against you. To accomplish his plan, he attacks in three vital areas of your life.

**His primary attack point is your purpose!**

Why is that his objective? Your purpose reflects the original meaning for your existence. It is the end which justifies the means—the destination that prompts the journey—the why that explains the reason. The devil understands that those who don't know where they are going will probably end up somewhere else.

> *Your occupation, your relationships and the events of your life may change, but your reason for being never will.*

Writer T.T. Munger states, "There is no road to success but through a clear strong purpose. Nothing can take its place. A purpose underlies character. It underlies culture. It underlies position. It underlies the attainment of every sort."

Every man is on a search for significance. We have all asked questions like, "Why am I here? What is the reason for my being?"

Scripture answers those questions when it declares, "You are worthy, our Lord and God, to receive glory and honor and power, for you created all things, and by your will they were created and have their being" (Revelation 4:11).

Even though it is difficult for us to fully comprehend, we were created for God's divine plan. English clergyman Jonathan Swift once wrote:

> ***"It is in men as in soils when there is a vein of gold that the owner knows not of."***

Certainly we are here for spiritual reasons, but God also had an objective in mind when He gave us a physical body. He desires that we become the person He has purposed for us to be.

The Apostle Paul wrote, "Therefore, I urge you, brothers, in view of God's mercy, to offer your bodies as living sacrifices, holy and pleasing to God—this is your spiritual act of worship" (Romans 12:1).

Why does the Lord want us to present ourselves totally to Him? So that He can help us accomplish His purpose for our lives. "Do not conform any longer to the pattern of this world, but be transformed by the renewing of your mind. Then you will be able to test and approve what God's will is—His good, pleasing and perfect will" (Romans 12:2).

Unfortunately, millions of well-meaning people have misplaced focus for their lives. They believe that talent, position, and personal accomplishments are all that truly matter. As a result, their actions—what they do—becomes the primary objective. They fail to hear God saying, "Your purpose is to, first of all, become the person I've created you to become."

Satan is not only evil, he is devious. The devil uses our talents to sidetrack us. He knows how the good can become the robber of the best.

> *Nothing pleases Satan more than to see us become so self-absorbed in our own interests that we ignore God's design for our life.*

Instead of spending your days on this earth in a fruitless search for material gain and personal power, use your God-given mind to seek His objective. Scripture declares, "Counsel in the heart of man is like deep water, But a man of understanding will draw it out" (Proverbs 20:5 NKJV).

## Reasons for Attack

Why does the devil attack your purpose? There are three basic reasons.

**First, Satan knows you were created for a reason.**

The Evil One fully understands that God has a grand strategy that includes you and me. We may not grasp the significance of it, but the devil certainly does. He knows that what happens in God's kingdom is not by accident or chance. The Lord has a specific plan and an eternal design.

**Second, Satan knows that God will use anything and everything in your life to accomplish His purpose.**

So often we look at events and say, "Why is this happening? It seems so wrong!" But God uses everything—even attacks of Satan—for our good. "And we know that all things work together for good to them that love God, and to them who are the called according to his purpose" (Romans 8:28 KVJ).

It's been said that if we keep our head and our heart going in the right direction we won't need to worry about our feet. Scripture says, "In all thy ways acknowledge him, and he shall direct thy paths" (Proverbs 3:6 KJV).

**Third, Satan knows that within your purpose lies your potential.**

In the inner resources of each of us resides promise and capacity that is virtually untapped. I'm not speaking of a specific task or the things you do, but the potential of what you can become for God.

The Lord spoke through Jeremiah, saying, "Before I formed you in the womb I knew you, before you were born I set you apart; I appointed you as a prophet to the nations" (Jeremiah 1:5).

Those words were not only for an Old Testament prophet, or for the coming Messiah, they are for you and me.

## What is Your Mission?

We often quote the scripture, "Where there is no vision, the people perish" (Proverbs 29:18 KJV), but without a knowledge of your ultimate purpose you will never understand God's dream for your life.

- Without purpose there can be no vision.
- Without vision there is no commitment.
- Without commitment there is no joy.
- And without joy there is no fulfillment.

I'm sure you have met people who are constantly chasing a new job, moving to a new location, searching for another relationship, or looking for another church. They cannot seem to find fulfillment. Why are they searching? They do not understand the mission for their life.

God's purpose was revealed to Adam through a garden. The Bible says, "The Lord God took the man and put him in the Garden of Eden to work it and take care of it" (Genesis 2:15).

Simply by following God's directive, he could have anything he desired. Yet Satan knew the bullet he could use to hinder Adam's purpose. He focused on the Tree of Knowledge rather than the Tree of Life. As a result, all of mankind suffered because of his actions.

God's purpose was revealed to Noah by an ark. The old man had never built a boat before, however this was the reason Noah was born. The critics exclaimed, "You're a fool!" Noah focused on the Ark, which represented salvation, rather than allowing his critics to cause him agitation.

- Abraham's purpose was revealed in a promise.
- Moses' purpose was revealed in a command.
- David's purpose was revealed in an anointing.
- Solomon's purpose was revealed in wisdom.
- Jesus' purpose was revealed at the Cross.

## THE POWER OF A DREAM

Do you remember the story of Joseph? God's intention for him was revealed in a dream.

Can you imagine a seventeen year old telling his older brothers and his family, "Listen to this dream I had: We were binding sheaves of grain out in the field when suddenly my sheaf rose and stood upright, while your sheaves gathered around mine and bowed down to it" (Genesis 37:6,7).

His brothers, who were already jealous because they thought he was their father's favorite, immediately asked, "Do you intend to reign over us? Will you actually rule us?" (v.8)

Joseph's brothers thought, "How arrogant. Who does he think he is?" They sold him into slavery in Egypt.

The events in his life changed drastically and by a miracle, Joseph became second in power to Potiphar, one of Pharaoh's officials. Then after being falsely accused by Potiphar's wife, the young man was sent to prison for thirteen years. He wondered, "How is this going to work for good?"

While Joseph was a prisoner, Pharaoh heard about his God-given ability to interpret dreams and called for him. Not only did Joseph fully explain the king's dream, but Pharaoh declared, "You shall be in charge of my palace, and all my people are to submit to your orders. Only with respect to the throne will I be greater than you." (Genesis 41:40).

Because of a great famine in Canaan, Joseph's brothers came to Egypt to plead for food. He disguised himself as they bowed before him, fulfilling God's original dream.

Joseph removed himself from their presence and wept as he realized that God's intention for his life was being made clear.

When Joseph finally made himself known to his brothers, he said, "But God sent me ahead of you to preserve for you a remnant on earth and to save your lives by a great deliverance. So then, it was not you who sent me here, but God. He made me father to Pharaoh, lord of his entire household and ruler of all Egypt" (Genesis 45:7, 8).

In the midst of a great crisis, God had an ultimate plan for Joseph.

## Your Mandate

Your family or your friends may not understand your reason for being, but that is not their responsibility. It is a matter between you and your Heavenly Father.

> *We often find ourselves on the wrong path because we seek the approval of others rather than the will of God.*

It is not important that your associates give their approval to what God is saying directly to you. They may never understand it. Your mandate is simply to be obedient.

Over and over the Lord has impressed upon me that it is no one else's responsibility to understand the unique blueprint God has revealed for my life. It is for me, and me alone.

We don't need to become apprehensive about what people think or say. They don't understand. In reality, the world is not attacking us, but rather the devil is assailing the purpose that God has placed on our life.

At times you may feel lonely and perhaps misunderstood, but God "rewards those who earnestly seek him" (Hebrews 11:6). We must choose daily to stay on purpose.

**Satan not only attacks your purpose, he wages a battle against your peace!**

Who is the Prince of Peace? Jesus Christ. Is it any wonder that the enemy wants you to live in conflict and turmoil?

Recently, a man spoke to me after a seminar and said, "Keith, I need you to add me to your prayer list. I don't know what the problem is, but I am so restless I can hardly sleep at night."

"That's probably a good sign," I told him.

"Why?" he inquired.

"When the Lord is about to do something great, the devil gets worried," I assured him. "Satan does everything in his power to attack your peace."

Claim the fact that Jesus came to calm the troubled water. In the midst of the storm, He said, "Peace, be still."

Tell Satan to stop his torment. Claim God's promise that: "The peace of God, which passeth all understanding, shall keep your hearts and minds through Christ Jesus" (Philippians 4:7).

Peace is priceless. This is why the devil attacks us in this specific area. Peacelessness comes by our getting off purpose. Peace is a byproduct of being on purpose.

## CREATED TO PROSPER

**Just as the devil targets your purpose and your peace, he also attacks your prosperity!**

You may ask, "Keith, is God really concerned about my success?"

Absolutely.

The person who delights in the law of the Lord, "is like a tree planted by streams of water, which yields its fruit in season and whose leaf does not wither. Whatever he does prospers" (Psalm 1:3).

What does the next verse say? "Not so the wicked! They are like chaff that the wind blows away." (Psalms 1:4).

It is God's will that His people thrive and prosper—spiritually, physically and materially. The Bible makes that plain when it states, "Beloved, I wish above all things that thou mayest prosper and be in health, even as thy soul prospereth" (3 John 1:2 KJV).

The devil has plans and attacks, but his schemes will not prevail. "For this purpose the Son of God was manifested, that he might destroy the works of the devil" (1 John 3:8 KJV). As the great missionary statesman Oswald J. Smith stated, "Everything the devil does, God over-reaches to serve His own purpose."

Not only did Christ die for us; if we receive His love and forgiveness we are free from our sin.

The Lord has given us a reason for our existence. He created us for His glory and desires that we live in victory. While Satan continues to plot and scheme, we can rest with this assurance: If God is for us, who can be against us?

CHAPTER 3

# CANCER OF THE SPIRIT

*Our adversary is a master strategist, forever fogging up our minds with smokescreens.*
— Charles Swindoll

The devil has a vast arsenal of weapons to use against you, but what is his ultimate, number one secret weapon?

- Is it some large external force he will suddenly throw into your path?
- Is it a circumstance such as health or finances that brings havoc to your life?
- Is it a harmful act he encourages someone to commit against you?
- Is it the result of spiritual wickedness in high places?

Each of these have the potential for serious consequences, but Satan's ultimate weapon against you is a cancer of the spirit that can be described in one word:

## Negativity

I call negativity "cancer of the spirit" because it is the silent killer of your spirit man.

The devil attacks you at your weakest point—your attitude. By inflicting an evil virus of criticism, pessimism, suspicion and doubt, he can destroy you from the inside out.

One day as I was reading the book of Numbers, I was astounded at how Satan caused a negative spirit to invade the children of Israel. It is one of the most over-looked stories in the Old Testament.

After spending several months in the region of Mount Sinai, the people, led by Moses, set out for the Promised Land. An event in the desert, however, had a disastrous effect on their adventure.

From inside Moses' own household, Miriam and Aaron—his brother and sister—openly began to questions his leadership.

Scripture records that "Miriam and Aaron spake against Moses because of the Ethiopian woman whom he married" (Numbers 12:1 KJV).

"'Has the Lord spoken only through Moses?" they asked. "Hasn't he also spoken through us?" And the Lord heard this" (v.2).

Their negative remarks were not only heard by those around them, but the Lord was listening too—and He was not pleased.

## AN ANGRY GOD

It is obvious that Moses was chosen by God, yet he was also a man—and no one knew his faults and weaknesses better than his own family.

Miriam, who was eighty years old, believed she had enough wisdom and understanding to state her opinion. She thought, "He may be the leader of the children of Israel, but he is my brother and I can't believe he married that woman!"

God didn't waste any time to express His displeasure. "At once the Lord said to Moses, Aaron and Miriam, Come out to the Tent of Meeting, all three of you.' So the three of them came out" (v.4)

The Lord descended in a pillar of cloud and stood at the entrance of the Tent and summoned Aaron and Miriam. When they both stepped forward, God said, "Listen to my words: When a prophet of the Lord is among you, I reveal myself to him in visions, I speak to him in dreams. But this is not true of my servant Moses; he is faithful in all my house. With him I speak face to face, clearly and not in riddles; he sees the form of the Lord" (vv. 6-8).

> *Then God asked this penetrating question: "Why then were you not afraid to speak against my servant Moses?" He was saying, "Do you not understand? This is my chosen one!" The Bible states that "The anger of the Lord burned against them, and he [God] left them". (v.9)*

What happened next is a vivid picture of what the Lord thinks of a negative spirit. "When the cloud lifted from above the Tent, there stood Miriam—leprous, like snow. Aaron turned toward her and saw that she had leprosy; and he said to Moses, "Please, my lord, do not hold against us the sin we so foolishly committed" (vv. 10-11).

Aaron became contrite. He pleaded, "Do not let her be like a stillborn infant coming from its mother's womb with its flesh half eaten away" (v.12).

What was Moses' response? He didn't say, "She deserves to be punished by God!" That was not his spirit. Instead, Moses cried out to the Lord, "O God, please heal her!" (v.13)

God replies to Moses, "If her father had spit in her face, would she not have been in disgrace for seven days?

Confine her outside the camp for seven days; after that she can be brought back" (v.14)

Miriam was confined outside the camp for a full week and the children of Israel did not continue their journey until she was brought back into the camp.

## WHAT WAS THE SIN?

Miriam and Aaron were guilty of a trespass that is rarely discussed from the pulpits of our land.

What was Aaron talking about when he said, "Forgive us of this sin?" God did not declare there was any specific iniquity of which they were guilty. He didn't say "You have committed adultery," or "You have lied." He didn't name one of the Ten Commandments that had been violated. Yet Aaron knew in his heart they had done something terribly wrong. This is why he cried to Moses, "Please don't hold this sin against us."

What was the transgression? It was negativity.

> *I have been in the church all of my life and am convinced that the body of Christ does not understand the seriousness of this issue.*

Some will say, "What's the harm? Everyone is entitled to state their opinion."

I wish I could tell you that the lessons learned by Miriam and Aaron were so profound that it transformed the children of Israel into positive, affirming people. Unfortunately, that's not the nature of a critical spirit. It is like a web that pulls everyone into its trap.

That becomes obvious when you look at the events which followed.

## God's Promise Hindered

When the children of Israel moved to an encampment in the desert of Paran, the Lord instructed Moses to send a group of men to spy out the land of Canaan—which God had promised to give to the Israelites. From each of the twelve ancestral tribes he was to send one of its leaders.

Moses told them, "Go up through the Negev and on into the hill country. See what the land is like and whether the people who live there are strong or weak, few or many. What kind of land do they live in? Is it good or bad? What kind of towns do they live in? Are they unwalled or fortified? How is the soil? Is it fertile or poor? Are there trees on it or not? Do your best to bring back some of the fruit of the land. (It was the season for the first ripe grapes.)" (Numbers 13:17-20).

The twelve spies explored the land as far as Hebron, where the descendants of Anak lived—they were men of great size that brought fear and terror to everyone who saw them.

As they passed through the Valley of Eschol, "they cut off a branch bearing a single cluster of grapes. Two of them carried it on a pole between them, along with some pomegranates and figs" (v.23).

After forty days of exploration, they returned to Moses and gave a full report of their experience to the entire assembly. "We went into the land to which you sent us," they announced, "and it does flow with milk and honey! Here is its fruit" (v.27).

> ***Canaan was everything God had promised—and more. They said, "Look, we have proof."***

That was the good news. Immediately, however, they began to express their fears and anxiety. "But the people who live there are powerful, and the cities are fortified and very large. We even saw descendants of Anak there" (v.28). In other words, "We saw the giants!"

Two of the spies, Joshua and Caleb, saw it differently. Caleb stood before Moses and the people and declared, "We should go up and take possession of the land, for we can certainly do it" (v.30).

The others, however, were filled with doubt and disbelief. They retorted, "We can't attack those people; they are stronger than we are. And they spread among the Israelites a bad report about the land they had seen. They said, "The land we explored devours those living in it. All the people we saw there are of great size" (vv.31-32).

Their self-esteem had fallen so low that they declared, "We seemed like grasshoppers in our own eyes, and we looked the same to them." (v.33).

They had fallen into the trap of destructive thinking that causes us to believe that the opinion we have of ourselves is how we expect others to see us.

## The Evil Report

Why do I call negativity "cancer of the spirit?" The words spoken by Miriam and Aaron in Numbers 12 permeated the thinking of the Children of Israel. Before this time, even in the midst of deplorable circumstances, the people said, "We're going to make it! The promised land will be ours!"

- They had been spared from the plagues of Egypt.
- They had seen the waters of the Red Sea miraculously part.
- They were fed with manna that fell from heaven.
- They drank water that began to flow from a dry rock.

Now a horrible spirit had been unleashed. Not only did they distrust Moses; now all they could see ahead were giants and defeat.

What happened when the children of Israel heard the report? "That night all the people of the community raised their voices and wept aloud" (Numbers 14:1).

Negativity breeds distress, depression, anger and hopelessness. They cried because of an evil report. This is why God hates this spirit so much. It is the cancer that kills faith.

Not only did they hear it, they believed it. "All the Israelites grumbled against Moses and Aaron, and the whole assembly said to them, "If only we had died in Egypt! Or in this desert!" (v.2)

"This is ridiculous," they complained. "At least back there we knew what was happening. Under Pharaoh we were comfortable and knew the rules. Here we have to trust God and live by faith."

> *The children of Israel were ready to retreat to security, even if it was bondage.*

In the desert, the people murmured, "Why is the Lord bringing us to this land only to let us fall by the sword? Our wives and children will be taken as plunder. Wouldn't it be better for us to go back?" (v.3). They said to each other, "We should choose a leader and go back to Egypt" (v.4).

Without question, they thought, "If Moses can't be trusted by his own family, why should we trust him?"

## Two Who Believed

In a dramatic moment, Moses and Aaron fell face down in front of the entire assembly. Joshua and Caleb—who had been with the twelve that spied out the land of Canaan—stepped forward. They tore their clothes and shouted. "The land we passed through and explored is exceedingly good. If the Lord is pleased with us, he will lead us into that land, a land flowing with milk and honey, and will give it to us" (vv.7-8).

Surrounded by a sea of skepticism, Joshua and Caleb warned the people, "Do not rebel against the Lord. And do not be afraid of the people of the land, because we will swallow them up…the Lord is with us" (v.9).

What was God's promise to these two leaders who did not lose their hope? They would not only survive, they would personally live to see Israel inhabit the Promised Land. Scripture declares, "The men Moses had sent to explore the land, who returned and made the whole community grumble against him by spreading a bad report about it…were struck down and died of a plague before the Lord" (vv.36-37).

This is how God views those who spread doubt and fear.

I was recently asked, "Why did Miriam suffer such grave consequences, and not Aaron?"

The answer rests in the fact that Aaron asked for forgiveness, but Miriam never did. She was not the one who pleaded with Moses, "Please do not hold this sin against us."

Perhaps she could have been spared from leprosy. Maybe she could have avoided the disgrace and humiliation of being sent outside of the camp. Scripture does not record that she ever said, "Will you please forgive me?"

> *You may not be inflicted with a*
> *visible disease, yet Satan wants*
> *to sap your power and potential*
> *through a negative spirit.*

How will you react when you see giants on the horizon? Will you be paralyzed by a negative spirit? Don't listen to the devil, who would have you say, "They are so big, and I am so small."

The Lord desires that you stand tall and tell the world, "Without Him I can do nothing. With Him, all things are possible."

CHAPTER 4

# WHERE DOES IT BEGIN?

*Satan wastes no ammunition on those who are dead in trespasses and sins.*
— Corrie ten Boom

Following the shocking tragedy of the Oklahoma City bombing and the senseless killing of sixteen children in Dunblane, Scotland, many people have struggled with the question, "Why would a good, loving, God allow something like this to happen?" They ask the question in a hundred ways, but still there seems to be no answer.

Several years ago the book, *"Why Bad Things Happen to Good People"*, made it to the top of the New York Times bestseller list. There are many events in life we simply cannot explain. Instead of asking "Why did this happen?" we should say, "It happened. How will I respond?" The primary issue is this: What are good people going to do when bad things happen?

You do not need to ask "Why?" A bomb or bullet does not change the fact that God is still God and He is sovereign.

Even if the guilty person writes a note or confesses, "This is why I did it," the proclamation doesn't change history. If someone with a psychological disorder blows up a building or shoots down innocent children, does it make any difference whether or not you understand the reason?

On a personal level, we constantly search for reasons. "Why did she say that about me?" Or, "Why would he treat me in such a horrible way?"

> *Satan loves it when we start asking "Why?" He knows it is the first step to a negative spirit.*

The moment we begin to doubt and question, the devil says, "Yes, keep asking "Why?" He knows that when we are looking for natural solutions we may even start to blame God. That is part of the devil's shrewd scheme.

Don't be deceived into questioning God's divine plan. There are certain mysteries that will never be revealed this side of eternity.

As the prince and power of the air, Satan's objective is to imprison you in his dungeon of darkness.

That will happen to those who continue to live in their sin, but as a born again child of God, you know that Satan no longer has power over you. The Word declares, "Greater is he that is in you, than he that is in the world." (1 John 4:4 KJV)

In the midst of such darkness, there came a light. His name is Jesus. Today the truth is shining through His church and through those who have been redeemed.

## WILL WE LISTEN?

Few people understand negativity. Even the dictionary gives it this hazy definition: "The opposite of being positive."

Psychologists describe negativism as "an attitude characterized by ignoring or opposing suggestions or orders from others, most often manifested in children."

From my observations, however, it is equally prevalent in grown men and women. How old was Miriam when she criticized her brother? Eighty!

I've heard people say, "If my boss thinks he is going to run my life, he's got another thing coming!" And I have listened to executives say the same thing about their employees. "Nobody's going to tell me what to do!"

The older we become the more difficult it is for someone to exercise power over us. It is especially true when the directive comes from the Almighty through one of His imperfect servants. I've listened to seasoned Christians complain, "If God wants to tell me something, He will do it directly. I don't need a go-between."

## From a Tiny Seed

Like a living plant, negativity is characterized by three distinct elements. It begins with a seed, it grows roots, and it produces fruit.

**1. The seed of negativity is rebellion.**

Every tree starts with a tiny seed, whether it produces lovely flowers or bitter fruit.

What is the seed that germinates into a negative spirit? It is rebellion.

I meet many Christians who continue to behave like adolescents. If there is the slightest problem, it suddenly becomes a mountain—not only in the church, but within their own families. When their children behave in a negative manner they immediately lash out in anger. Often, God will use our children's behavior to speak to us about our own behavior.

Rebellion expresses itself in fault-finding. As Zig Ziglar states,

> *"Some people find fault like there is a reward for it."*

Looking for the mistakes of others is a diversion that keeps us from doing what we should—and becoming what we could.

In the past decade, God has opened doors that have allowed me to speak in person to several million young people. Not only have I talked to them from the platform of school assemblies or at large youth rallies, I have spent hundreds of hours dealing with teens face to face.

Can I tell you why young people rebel? It is because they hear their parents say one thing and see them doing the exact opposite! As a fourteen-year-old girl in Oklahoma told me, "Why should I go to church? My mom and dad are there every time the doors open, yet they constantly criticize the preacher and tear down every member of the congregation."

Many people rebel because of insecurity. Often, the person we are depending on for strength and support disappoints us. The individual who has been our role mode—our "ideal"—bursts our bubble. We suddenly feel vulnerable and uncertain.

- Our parents have fallen from their lofty pedestal.
- The mate we have chosen for life is not living up to our expectations.
- Our employer has betrayed our trust.
- Our church is filled with "hypocrites."

How do most people respond to such disappointments? Instead of seeing themselves as agents of change, they become defiant and begin to rebel. Because of their own insecurity, they begin building walls around themselves and erecting bars and barricades. Without realizing what has happened, they become prisoners of their own negativity.

*We all have the tendency to judge others by their actions, yet we judge ourselves by our intent.*

We rationalize, "Even though I didn't accomplish it, I intended to!" That's why we are tough on those around us, but rarely scold ourselves.

Since all things begin with a seed, do not allow rebellion to germinate in the soil of your spirit.

**2. The roots of negativity are jealousy and bitterness.**

Scripture records that Lucifer was cast out of heaven because of his jealousy. He wanted to be greater than the Almighty.

Satan bragged, "I will ascend to heaven; I will raise my throne above the stars of God; I will sit enthroned on the mount of the assembly, on the utmost heights of the sacred mountain. I will ascend above the tops of the clouds; I will make myself like the Most High" (Isaiah 14:13-14).

Because of those roots of envy, the devil was literally kicked out of heaven. "How you have fallen from heaven... You have been cast down to the earth; you who once laid low the nations... You are brought down to the grave, to the depths of the pit" (vv.12, 15).

When you allow the seed of rebellion to be nourished through the roots of jealousy and bitterness, you align yourself with Satan.

Have you ever listened to negative people?

- "I don't know why he got that promotion. I work just as hard!"
- "Just because she drives an expensive car, she thinks she's something special!"
- "I'd be popular too if my dad was the bank president."

What is the common denominator? Jealousy—which leads to bitterness. When those two evil roots begin to sprout, a monster has been unleashed.

By dwelling on the success of others rather than our own potential, we develop a poverty mentality filled with envy and resentment. As a result, we make it easy for Satan to take a stronghold on our life.

**3. The fruit of negativity is a critical spirit.**

Even though I wasn't a preacher's kid, I grew up on the pew of a church. My father was a Dallas policeman and my mother sang in the choir. When the church doors were open, we were always present.

As a child, a teen, an adult and now as a minister, I have observed the critical spirit that has been unleashed upon the church. I believe it comes from the depths of hell itself.

It is a universal law that what we plant and grow will bear fruit. Negativity doesn't stay hidden; it produces a harvest. What is the crop of negativity? It is a spirit of criticism, condemnation and reproach.

> *Spreading an evil report doesn't happen by accident. It is the outgrowth of a corrupt seed that has broken through the soil of your spirit and has sprouted.*

Satan is critical about God and everything that is Holy. He is also judgmental of you and shows his devilish grin every time you fail. How does scripture describe Satan?

- He is a deceiver (Revelation 12:9).
- He is the accuser of the brethren (Revelation 12:10).
- He is a liar and the father of lies (John 8:44).

When people are negative about you, consider the source. It is the result of something that has been planted within them by Satan—the one who has fallen from grace and cast into eternal darkness. He is the originator of all condemnation.

People may yield to the devil's temptation and harm you with unkind words, but remember God loves you and has prepared a divine plan for your life. Why are you under attack? Satan does not want God's ultimate purpose to be fulfilled.

## Looking at the Heart

Perhaps the most important test for a negative spirit is how we treat those the Lord has chosen to minister to us.

When God anoints a leader, that man or woman deserves our support, not our backbiting, scorn or criticism. The person selected is not our choice, but the Lord's.

God was searching for someone to replace King Saul when He told Samuel, "I am sending you to Jesse of Bethlehem. I have chosen one of his sons to be king" (1 Samuel 16:1).

Jesse and his sons were present at a special sacrifice, and when Samuel saw his oldest son, Eliab, he thought "Surely, he is the one."

Samuel was surprised when God told him, "Do not consider his appearance or his height, for I have rejected him. The Lord does not look at the things man looks at. Man looks at the outward appearance, but the Lord looks at the heart" (1 Samuel 16:7).

After seven of Jesse's sons came before Samuel, he said "The Lord has not chosen these…Are these all the son's you have?" (vv. 10-11)

"There is still the youngest," Jesse answered, "but he is tending the sheep."

God chose the least likely candidate, little David, to become king of Israel.

It doesn't matter what the circumstances in your life may be. God is God, and when He chooses you, there is no need to ask "Why?"

**When the Lord becomes your Master, miracles begin to happen.**

- Seeds of rebellion can become seeds of righteousness.
- Roots of jealousy and bitterness can be traded for roots of joy and blessing.
- Your critical spirit can be exchanged for the fruit of the Spirit.

Ask God for that transformation to start today.

Others may see a shepherd boy, but God sees a King.

CHAPTER 5

# THE REVEALING RESULTS

*Words: Do you fully understand their power? Can any of us really grasp the mighty force behind the things we say?*
— *Joni Eareckson Tada*

As a father, I know how much children love it when someone reads them a story. One fable, in particular, always holds their attention. It is the story of a wooden puppet named Pinocchio.[1]

You probably recall that Pinocchio told the Fairy a tale of how he fell into the hands of thieves. "What did you do with the four gold pieces?" he was asked.

"I lost them," replied Pinocchio. But he told a lie, because he had them concealed in his pocket.

The moment he said this, his nose grew four inches longer.

"Where did you lose them?" continued the Fairy. He replied, "In the forest near here."

At this second lie, his nose grew still longer.

When a search of the forest was about to begin Pinocchio changed his story. "I did not lose the coins; I swallowed them when I took my medicine."

Another lie and the puppet's nose grew so long that he couldn't turn around.

Eventually, when he learned the lesson that he must always tell the truth, he was transformed from a wooden toy into a real live boy. In the story, the man named Giuseppe became his father, not just the clock worker who had invented him in the first place.

This fable crosses my mind every time I think about what kind of narrative could be written to teach young children about the dangers of negativity.

What would happen to the main character, who always tears people down, rather than build them up? What would be the result of speaking harmful words?

> *Try to picture this. Every time the person speaks a critical word his tongue would suddenly grow longer.*

People would ask, "Sir, what is wrong with your tongue?"

He would have to tell them, "This is the result of being negative."

Eventually the man's tongue would be hanging out of his mouth like an elephant's trunk and he would barely be able to speak. The situation would reach the point that he would have to push a wheelbarrow carrying his tongue everywhere he went.

Perhaps that implausible story would hammer home the point that critical words produce dreadful results. We need to look at this problem for what it really is, a disease. Or, to say it another way, a dis-ease, since it makes life so uncomfortable.

## What Does it Mean?

Recently, while my wife and I were in a restaurant, I borrowed a crayon from the waitress and wrote the word N-E-G-A-T-I-V-I-T-Y down the side of a scrap of paper. I then gave a definition to each letter of the acrostic.

Here's what I believe the letters represent:

**N**— **Never-prospering.**

> The person who is overtaken by a pessimistic spirit is mortgaging their future. In effect, every critical word uttered becomes a liability rather than an asset. Before long, those words become a mountain of debt under which we are buried.

The prophet Zechariah stood before the people and declared, "This is what God says: Why do you disobey the Lord's commands? You will not prosper. Because you have forsaken the Lord, he has forsaken you" (2 Chronicles 24:20).

What will happen if you do not follow the commands of the Lord? "You will be unsuccessful in everything you do; day after day you will be oppressed and robbed, with no one to rescue you" (Deuteronomy 28:29).

Remember, success begins with significance understood.

## E— Error-finding.

I'm certain you have encountered those who believe it is their mission in life to find fault with everyone they meet. Scripture does not deal lightly with such people. As the prophet Isaiah wrote: "For the fool speaks folly, his mind is busy with evil: He practices ungodliness and spreads error concerning the Lord" (Isaiah 32:6).

What is the danger of being judgmental? We are judged ourselves. In His Sermon on the Mount, Jesus asked, "Why do you look at the speck of sawdust in your brother's eye and pay no attention to the plank in your own eye? How can you say to your brother, 'Let me take the speck out of your eye,' when all the time there is a plank in your own eye?" (Matthew 7:3-4).

Jesus gave the solution when He declared, "You hypocrite, first take the plank out of your own eye, and then you will see clearly to remove the speck from your brother's eye" (v.5).

## G — Guile-conniving.

In almost every instance, people who have a negative spirit are also filled with guile and deceit. They constantly manipulate and connive to get their own way.

Referring to those whose lives are filled with pretense, Jeremiah wrote, "Their tongue is a deadly arrow; it speaks with deceit. With his mouth each speaks cordially to his neighbor, but in his heart he sets a trap for him." (Jeremiah 9:8)

Being known for craftiness is not an attribute, but a badge of dishonor. The Word warns us: "Rid yourselves of all malice and all deceit, hypocrisy, envy, and slander of every kind" (1 Peter 2:1).

## A — Accusation-throwing.

The devil is delighted when you bring accusations against your neighbor — and against God. As the "accuser of the brethren" (Revelation 12:10) he will do whatever it takes to bring you down to his level.

Since Satan has been assigned to hell forever, he retaliates against the Almighty through you. By accusing you—a child of God—he is actually denouncing the Lord.

Throughout Scripture, men and women of faith have been falsely charged. Often, however, the accusations backfire. For example, in Daniel's day, "At the king's command, the men who had falsely accused Daniel were brought in and thrown into the lions' den, along with their wives and children. And before they reached the floor of the den, the lions overpowered them and crushed all their bones" (Daniel 6:24).

## T— Tale-bearing.

Have you noticed that people who dwell on the negative are bearers of rumor and hearsay? Many actually thrive on scandal and pass it on almost quicker than it arrives. The writer of Proverbs says, "The words of a gossip are like choice morsels; they go down to a man's inmost parts" (Proverbs 18:8).

What outcome can we expect from a rumormonger? "A perverse man stirs up dissension, and a gossip separates close friends" (Proverbs 16:28).

The Psalmist asked the Lord, "Who may dwell in your sanctuary? Who may live on your holy hill?" (Psalms15:1).

Here is the answer: "He whose walk is blameless and who does what is righteous, who speaks the truth from his heart and has no slander on his tongue, who does his neighbor no wrong and casts no slur on his fellowman" (w. 2-3).

Vow to eliminate tale-bearing from your conversation.

## I— Idolatry-worshiping.

A major reason the enemy entices us into this trap is so that we will lose our trust in God. By causing us to question Scripture and doubt our faith, he leads us down a path of unbelief and unveils substitutes for God—idols of his choosing.

You might say, "I don't have a statue in my house or a false god sitting in my back yard."

Are you sure? Anything we place before the Lord becomes an idol, whether it be a shiny boat we take to the lake on Sunday morning, our occupation, or the size of our bank account. Even your opinion can be held in such high esteem that it becomes paramount.

Why did the children of Israel have such a problem with idolatry? Because they became extremely negative. They failed to heed the commandment

God delivered at Mount Sinai, "You shall have no other gods before me" (Exodus 20:3).

Paul warned us not to associate with anyone "who calls himself a brother but is ... an idolater or a slanderer, a drunkard or a swindler" (1 Corinthians 5:11).

How should we respond when we recognize that something is becoming a wedge between us and the Lord? "Therefore, my dear friends, flee from idolatry" (1 Corinthians 10:14).

## V — Vision-killing.

What happens to the great vision the Lord has for our future? Why isn't it recognized and fulfilled?

Satan uses our tongues to abort God's vision within us before it is even birthed. He has us repeat the words, "I can't do that," and "I know I'll probably fail," so many times that we actually believe them.

A gentleman told me recently, "I feel I'm on a treadmill. I'm working hard, yet I don't seem to be getting anywhere."

Millions of God-fearing people try to do what is right but still feel unfulfilled. They need to realize that their life will have meaning only when their activities line up with God's unique purpose—not for others, but for them.

Yes, all things work together for good to those who love Him and "who have been called according to His purpose" (Romans 8:28).

God's plan for you is not cloudy, but clear. As He told Habakkuk, "Write the vision, and make it plain upon tables, that he may run that readeth it. For the vision is yet for an appointed time, but at the end it shall speak, and not lie: though it tarry, wait for it; because it will surely come, it will not tarry" (Habakkuk 2:2-3 KJV).

Don't allow Satan to kill the vision that God has for you.

## I— **Insecure-living.**

Fault-finding, critical people lack security. They mistakenly believe the only way to the top is by pulling others down. As a result, they stay at the lowest rung of the ladder.

I constantly encounter people who try to show their superiority by pointing out how others are inferior. Without realizing it, they are building a house on the wrong foundation. Confidence, both spiritual and personal, comes from a positive relationship with God and the knowledge that you have a pure, clean heart before Him.

Jesus gave reassurance to those who were filled with anxiety and insecurity, "Therefore I tell you, do not worry about your life, what you will eat or drink or about your body, what you will wear. Is not life more important than food, and the body more important than clothes?" (Matthew 6:25)

Then Christ spoke these great words: "But seek first His kingdom and his righteousness, and all these things will be given to you as well" (v.33).

That is the best security you will ever know.

## T— Tithe-robbing.

Many people journey through life and become like the Dead Sea. The waters flow into it from the Sea of Galilee through the Jordan River, but there it stops.

The Dead Sea is filled with salt and cannot sustain life. Why? Because it receives but does not give— there is not even a current.

Negative people fall into the same pattern. They become "takers" rather than "givers." Before long they are actually stealing from their Creator.

Through the prophet Malachi, the Lord asked, "Will a man rob God? Yet you rob me. But you ask, 'How do we rob you?' In tithes and offerings" (Malachi 3:8).

The Lord said "You are under a curse—the whole nation of you—because you are robbing me" (v.9).

What was the solution? "Bring the whole tithe into the storehouse, that there may be food in my house. Test me in this ... and see if I will not throw open the floodgates of heaven and pour out so much blessing that you will not have room enough for it" (v. 10).

Do you want to be showered with God's blessing? Develop a spirit of giving.

## Y — Yoke-bearing.

Those who live with a contrary, dissenting spirit are inviting a yoke to be placed on them. They become like the Psalmist, who wrote: "My guilt has overwhelmed me like a burden too heavy to bear" (Psalms 38:4).

Negativity is a sin and Christ stated, "Everyone who sins is a slave to sin" (John 8:34).

The burden, however, can be lifted and the bonds can be removed. The Lord declared, "Take my yoke upon you and learn from me, for I am gentle and humble in heart, and you will find rest for your souls. For my yoke is easy and my burden is light" (Matthew 11:28, 30).

We can stand in the liberty and freedom Christ has given "and be not entangled again with the yoke of bondage" (Galatians 5:1 KJV).

Why should your life be filled with error, guile, idolatry and accusations? The Lord has something far better for you. He is ready to give you a vision, pour out His abundance and lift your heavy burden.

The answer is found in one word: Jesus.

CHAPTER 6

# TRUTH OR CONSEQUENCES?

*Truthful lips endure forever, but a lying tongue lasts only a moment.*
*— Proverbs 12:19*

God doesn't take your actions lightly. For every cause there is an effect. For every act there is a result.

In chapter three we discussed how Moses' older brother and sister, Aaron and Miriam, turned against God's chosen leader. They disapproved of the woman he had decided to marry.

Not only is that story central to this message, but the aftermath of their actions cannot be ignored.

Perhaps Miriam believed she had earned the right to be critical. After all, she had protected Moses from the time of his birth.

When Pharaoh decreed that every Hebrew boy under the age of two must be killed, Moses was hidden in a papyrus basket his mother built for him. He floated in the reeds along the banks of the Nile.

Miriam watched from a distance as Pharaoh's daughter walked along the river bank and noticed the covered basket in the water. She opened it and saw the baby. He was crying, and she felt sorry for him. "This is one of the Hebrew babies," she said (Exodus 2:6).

Miriam approached Pharaoh's daughter and asked, "'Shall I go and get one of the Hebrew women to nurse the baby for you?'" (V.7). "'Yes, go,' she answered. And the girl went and got the baby's mother" (v.8).

As a result, Moses was raised in his own home-with his mother being a servant to Pharaoh's daughter.

Many years later, in the wilderness, Miriam may have felt justified in her criticism, but there was a price to pay.

Those who find fault and create dissension never win. There are both short-term and long-term repercussions.

## Short-Term Consequences

You won't have to wait for months or years to see the effects of negativity. Here are four results you can expect almost immediately.

### Short-term consequence #1: God's Anger.

Many believe the Lord's wrath is unleashed only when a grievous sin is committed. No. Those acts may cause Him great sadness and hurt, but His anger is released when we become negative and critical.

How did God respond when Miriam and Aaron spoke against Moses? "The anger of the Lord burned against them and he left them" (Numbers 12:9).

Later, the Psalmist recorded how the children of Israel "willfully put God to the test by demanding the food they craved" (Psalms 78:18). "When the Lord heard them, He was very angry; his fire broke out against Jacob, and his wrath rose against Israel" (v.21).

### Short-term consequence #2: God's chastisement.

A critical spirit invites the Lord's reproof, which can be both swift and severe. In Miriam's case, she became leprous-"like snow" (Numbers 12:10).

I believe that if Miriam had been quick to repent she would not have been inflicted with this dreaded disease. Aaron repented and was spared, but not his sister.

Why does God chastise us? Because He cares deeply and does not want us to stray from His will. As a father loves a son, the Lord loves those who are His sons and daughters.

### Short-term consequence #3:
### Immediate disempowerment.

The Lord has a way of letting us know who is in charge.

Miriam had been given the title "Mother of Israel", after the children of Israel had crossed through the Red Sea on dry land. She was the one who took the tambourine and timbrel and began to lead the people in worship.

Now, perhaps jealous that Moses was about to marry someone who might become a new "mother" to the nation, she criticized her brother. Her power was instantly taken away and she found herself cast outside the city.

### Short-term consequence #4:
### Alignment with Satan.

The moment we fall victim to a critical spirit, our words and actions are no longer in harmony with the Lord. Instead, we are aligned with the devil. We speak death rather than life. We curse rather than bless.

When we lift our voice against our brother, our sister, our pastor, or those who have been created in the image of God, we empower Satan against them.

Listen to the warning of the Apostle Paul: "I am afraid that just as Eve was deceived by the serpent's cunning, your minds may somehow be led astray from your sincere and pure devotion to Christ" (2 Corinthians 11:3).

# Long-Term Consequences

In addition to God's immediate response to negativity, there are also long-term effects. Here are seven areas in which your life can be permanently affected.

**Long-term consequence #1:**
**Fear.**

It's been said that "fear is the father of all failure." That is true. You can never have faith when you have fear.

It was not God, but rather the children of Israel who were fearful and wanted to scout out the land. As Moses stated, "Then all of you came to me and said, 'Let us send men ahead to spy out the land for us and bring back a report about the route we are to take and the towns we will come to" (Deuteronomy 1:22).

Since the Lord had already promised them the land, why was covert action necessary? It wasn't. They were acting on anxiety and fear.

Remember, God commands us to walk by faith, not by sight.

**Long-term consequence #2:**
**Inability to recognize what is valuable.**

If the children of Israel had truly recognized that the land of Canaan was of value, the obstacles in their way would not have mattered. When you know God's purpose for your life, the height of the walls or the giants you encounter become secondary.

When we become skeptical, it blinds us to what is truly valuable.

**Long-term consequence # 3:
An ungrateful spirit.**

Looking at the world through the eyes of doubt and pessimism produces an ungrateful spirit — what John Maxwell calls "the most unhealthy of all emotions."

The pomegranates brought back from Canaan could have been the size of watermelons. They could have been gold bars. Yes, the land God had promised was flowing with milk and honey, yet that did not seem to matter. The people were not grateful for where the Lord was taking them, because they had never been truly grateful for where He had taken them from.

**Long-term consequence #4:
Inability to have true joy.**

In my observations, people with a critical spirit live as though they are on a roller coaster. There may be a few high points on their journey, but as the ride continues, they fall lower and lower until they reach their final destination.

God did not create you for an "up and down" existence. Just as He placed the earth in its orbit, He has plans for your life to be steady and secure.

True happiness comes with the knowledge that you are God's child and He has all things in control. "The joy of The Lord is your strength" (Nehemiah 8:10).

**Long-term consequence #5:
Inability to truly succeed.**

An attitude of gloom and despair will destroy personal achievement. It is a road built by Satan that leads to the land of failure.

Did you know that it is God's plan for you to be a success? The Word declares, "The Lord will make you the head, not the tail. If you pay attention to the commands of the Lord…and carefully follow them, you will always be at the top, never at the bottom" (Deuteronomy 28:13).

**Long-term consequence #6:
Hindering, rather than helping people.**

The power of influence is universal. It will be used for good or for evil. Unfortunately, those mired in pessimism pull people into the same cesspool they have created. Their influence hinders rather than helps.

The words of dissension from Miriam and Aaron did not stay within the household. They spread like an infection and contaminated virtually all of the children of Israel. In fear, the people cried aloud, "If only we had died in Egypt!" (Numbers 14:2).

How do people feel after a conversation with you? Hopefully, they are encouraged and inspired.

**Long-term consequence #7:**
**Death to your potential.**

History records that over two million people embarked on the exodus to the Promised Land. How many reached Canaan? Only two—Joshua and Caleb.

God was serious when He said, "Not one of them will ever see the land I promised on oath to their forefathers. No one who has treated me with contempt will ever see it" (Numbers 14:23). The only exceptions were the two who brought back a positive report (v.30). God said, "Caleb has a different spirit and follows me wholeheartedly" (v.24). And Joshua told the people not to be afraid (v.9).

It took them 44 years, yet they made it! They focused on the solution, not the problem. They looked to God, not to the giants.

## The Bottom Line

The consequences of negativity are more than you or I were ever created to bear. By allowing the seed to germinate, you are opening the door to a lifetime of sorrow and heartache. What is the end result?

**First**: You will *see* in unbelief.

The picture you have of your world is the picture you have of yourself. Is it a reflection of belief or unbelief?

I often share the story of a pastor's little boy who kept interrupting his dad while he was trying to prepare his sermon on a Saturday afternoon. Finally, in frustration, the dad tore up a map of the world in small pieces and handed it to his son. He said, "Go and put the map of the world together. When you finish I'll give you a quarter."

The pastor thought, "Now I'll have the whole afternoon to study."

About ten minutes later his son returned with the map perfectly fitted together. "How did you do that so quickly?" asked the surprised dad.

"Oh, it was easy," replied his smiling son. "On the back of the map there was a picture of a man. When I put the man together, the world came together, too."

**Second**: You will *speak* in unbelief.

The enemy will use your words to kill the vision that God has for you. Like those who wandered in the desert, you will begin to see yourself as a grasshopper and say, "There's no way I can succeed."

*What you truly believe always
comes to the surface.*

Jesus declared, "A good man out of the good treasure of his heart bringeth forth that which is good; and an evil man out of the evil treasure of his heart bringeth forth that which is evil: for of the abundance of the heart his mouth speaketh" (Luke 6:45 KJV).

**Third: You will *act* in unbelief.**

When the children of Israel heard the evil report, they not only believed it, but it changed their behavior.

With loud voices they cried and murmured against Moses and wished they were dead. They even accused the Lord of deceiving them and began to rebel against God's chosen leadership.

Not only did the report produce fear and cowardice, it caused a spirit of violence and "the whole assembly talked about stoning [Moses and Aaron]" (Numbers 14:10).

Negativity affects everything about you — what you see, what you say, and your behavior. It deforms you spiritually.

You may ask, "What is the answer? Is it an affliction that has no cure? Is there hope?

There is a solution and that is what we are about to discover.

CHAPTER 7

# BREAKING THE ADDICTION

*I'm not afraid of the devil. The devil can handle me — he's got judo I've never heard of. But he can't handle the One to whom I'm joined; he can't handle the One to who I'm united; he can't handle the One whose nature dwells in my nature.*

*— A.W. Tozer*

Over the years I've heard sermons on the battle ground of our thought life, studied what Paul wrote concerning the "renewing of our mind," and even read Norman Vincent Peale's bestseller, *The Power of Positive Thinking*. However, I have still pondered these questions: "Where do thoughts come from?" "What is their origination?"

Let's try a quick experiment. What do you think about when I mention the color purple? Unless you are color blind you think about an eggplant, a violet, or something that is purple.

Is it possible that our thoughts come from words? Yes.

> *What we think about is the result of words that have been deposited—not only in our mind, but in the soil of our spirit.*

Immediately after Christ stated that "Out of the abundance of the heart the mouth speaks," He declared, "The good man brings good things out of the good stored up in him, and the evil man brings evil things out of the evil stored up in him. But I tell you that men will have to give account on the Day of Judgment for every careless word they have spoken. For by your words you will be acquitted, and by your words you will be condemned" (Matthew 12:35-37).

We know that:

- Our thoughts influence our emotions.
- Our emotions influence our actions.
- Our actions influence our habits.
- Our habits influence our character.
- Our character influences our destiny and the destiny of others.

What is not mentioned in this cycle, yet is at the core, is the power of the spoken word.

We are created in the image of the same God who spoke the world into existence. That means He has given us the ability to use that same creative force — the strength of our words, and the power of our tongue.

As we begin to speak either words of life or words of death, we are making permanent deposits in our spirit.

Let me illustrate.

I can go to a bank and say, "Hi, my name is Keith Craft, and I would like a million dollars. Would you please have that debited from my account?"

The banker would probably say, "How do you spell your last name?"

"C-R-A-F-T," I would tell him.

After punching a few numbers on his computer, he would say, "I'm sorry, Mr. Craft. We cannot give you that amount because our records indicate that you do not have a million dollars in your account."

Our spirit operates in the same way. What we have not planted is not available, but what has been spoken by our mouth is deposited deep within us.

When the Word takes root in our spirit it becomes effectual because it bypasses our mind and moves into the area of "knowing".

## Good or Evil?

On a parallel track with the authority of our words, there is an awesome power that resides in our tongue.

James paints this vivid picture: "When we put bits into the mouths of horses to make them obey us, we can turn the whole animal. Or take ships as an example. Although they are so large and are driven by strong winds, they are steered by a very small rudder wherever the pilot wants to go. Likewise the tongue is a small part of the body, but it makes great boasts. Consider what a great forest is set on fire by a small spark" (James 3:3-5).

He continues, "The tongue also is a fire, a world of evil among the parts of the body. It corrupts the whole person, sets the whole course of his life on fire, and is itself set on fire by hell. All kinds of animals, birds, reptiles and creatures of the sea are being tamed and have been tamed by man, but no man can tame the tongue. It is a restless evil, full of deadly poison" (vv. 6-8).

James' description is like a double-edge sword. With it, "we praise our Lord and Father, and with it we curse men, who have been made in God's likeness" (James 3:9).

In this revealing passage, there are <u>ten important things to remember</u> about the tongue:

1. It is a "small part of the body" (v. 5).
2. It boasts great things (v. 5).

3. It is "a fire" (v. 6).
4. It is "a world of evil" (v. 6).
5. It "corrupts the whole person" (v. 6).
6. It sets afire "the whole course of [our] life" (v. 6).
7. It is untamable (vv. 7-8).
8. It is "a restless evil" (v. 8).
9. It is "full of deadly poison" (v. 8).
10. It is used to praise God and curse men (v. 9).

This may seem like the ultimate paradox, yet we know that our tongue can be used as an instrument to bring honor to the Father and blessing to His children.

## A Self-Fulfilling Prophecy

Several years ago, I heard someone say, "Oh, don't listen to him. He's a negaholic!"

Before that time I had heard people described as alcoholics, drugoholics and sexoholics, but this was a new term. Now I've met hundreds of them—people "hooked" on pessimism to such a degree that they perpetually see the worst.

*Over time a negative habit can become an addiction that takes control of your thinking, your emotions and your behavior.*

It becomes much like compulsive overeating, drug abuse or anything else that is addictive by nature.

In his fascinating book, *You Can't Afford the Luxury of a Negative Thought*, Peter McWilliams says, "One of the easiest ways to be right is to predict failure—especially for yourself." Those who fall prey to that syndrome are victims of a self-fulfilling prophecy.

The reason something becomes an addiction is not only because of the emotional stimuli, but a physical stimulation in the form of an adrenalin rush — a chemical release that causes a craving for more.

Some people experience it through negativity, whether via the spoken word, the thought process, or through their actions. It not only becomes their reputation; it is their preferred lifestyle.

## Four Great Mistakes

How does a person become critical? How do they reach the point where they see a world filled with doom rather than deliverance?

We become negative as a result of these four basic errors.

## Mistake number one: Viewing the world through eyes of imperfection.

Once, after the children of Israel fled the clutches of Pharaoh they looked behind them and saw a huge cloud of dust caused by hundreds of approaching chariots, horses and Egyptian troops. The army was led by Pharaoh himself, hoping to capture the Hebrews because he realized that by letting these people go, his nation had lost their services.

Instead of being inspired by God's promise of a better tomorrow, they saw the world through their own eyes of imperfection and concluded they were about to die. The Bible says, "They were terrified" (Exodus 14:10).

That is what happens when we look at events through our limited perspective. Scripture declares, "The man without the Spirit does not accept the things that come from the Spirit of God, for they are foolishness to him, and he cannot understand them, because they are spiritually discerned" (1 Corinthians 2:14).

As believers, we no longer see the world through the eyes of imperfection. Why? Because "We have the mind of Christ" (v.16).

## Mistake number two: Focusing on the past.

General Douglas MacArthur once said, "Unless we learn the lessons of history we are doomed to repeat them."

However, there is a great difference between learning from the past and living there.

Great civilizations have come and gone. And in the 200 short years of our nation's existence we have seen the effects of moral decline on a society that was founded on biblical principles.

> *It's true. When you begin to deny God, you lose the very foundation on which morals exist. You become a value-less society.*

Does that mean we should constantly look behind us to the "good old days?" Absolutely not. Often times, the only reason the good old days are the good old days is because they are not here anymore. What God is preparing for the future is better than anything we've ever known.

Why did the children of Israel wander in the desert for over 40 years on a journey that was supposed to take only eleven days? They focused on their yesterday, not their tomorrow. They were saying, "Oh, if we could only return to being slaves to the Egyptians!"

Friend, there is not one verse in Scripture that says walking by faith is simple. And Satan is very much aware of that fact. That is why he wants us to look back, not ahead.

## Mistake number three: Magnifying the problems at hand.

If I were asked to name one thing that will never change, it would be this:

*You will always be faced with problems.*

That is not a doomsday message, but a reflection of fact. At certain times in our life we all face unforeseen difficulties that can involve relationships, finances or health.

Living in the "seen" realm, it is easy for us to magnify our problems rather than to maximize the solution.

The Israelites began to overstate the strength of their enemies. They dwelt on the fact that they had to eat manna instead of meat. They exaggerated the size of the giants and magnified the perils of the desert rather than seeing the strong hand of the Almighty.

## Mistake number four: Failing to trust in God.

Why do we become negative? In many cases it is because the Lord didn't work out our difficulties the way we thought He should.

As children, we learn to say, "Look, I can do it myself" and often become so self-sufficient we never turn to the Lord for help.

"In God we trust," is much more than a simple statement engraved on our coins. It must be the guiding principle that governs every action of our life. "In Him our hearts rejoice, for we trust in his holy name" (Psalms 33:21).

*Some people can have a "Red Sea" experience and be miraculously delivered from the hand of the enemy, yet they fail to rely on God as the total source of their supply.*

Scripture tells us the folly of placing trust in our weapons (Psalm 44:6), our wealth (Psalm 49:6-7), our works (Jeremiah 38:7), or our own righteousness (Ezekiel 33:13).

When obstacles loom larger than life itself, there is only one hope -only one trust. Remember the words of Christ: "With man this is impossible, but with God all things are possible" (Matthew 9:26).

The Lord not only erases our errors, He breaks the cycle of our past by giving us new thoughts, a new vocabulary, and a glorious new life.

CHAPTER 8

# THE CURE

*And Satan trembles when he sees
the weakest Saint upon his knees.*
— William Cowper

Like a rising river, it is almost impossible to escape the flood of negativity released by Satan. We turn and are confronted with conflict, tragedy and pain. We walk through a mall and hear people taking God's name in vain without apology. And, as these chapters have documented, the spirit of criticism and pessimism has invaded the church.

What is the solution for those on a downward spiral of dark thoughts and unhealthy emotions? Is there hope for the person who has become judgmental, resentful and filled with anxiety?

In today's chaotic climate can we really experience the fruit of the Spirit—"Love, joy, peace, patience, kindness, goodness, faithfulness, gentleness and self-control"? (Galatians 5:22-23)

## What's the Prescription?

If we are suffering from an illness, our physician will prescribe a remedy. But how do we deal with Satan's number one weapon against us —negativity? Where is the answer? What is the cure?

To me, here is what the letters **C-U-R-E** represent…

## C — Confess

The road to recovery begins when you acknowledge your faults and accept responsibility for your actions. You must not only confess it to yourself, but to those you may have harmed — and to God.

Follow the example of the Psalmist, who wrote: "Then I acknowledged my sin to you and did not cover up my iniquity. I said, 'I will confess my transgressions to the Lord' — and you forgave the guilt of my sin" (Psalms 32:5).

## U — Understand

It baffles me that some people live a negative life and wait for a positive outcome. That's impossible. As Albert Einstein said, "Insanity is doing the same things over and over and expecting different results."

Transformation begins with an understanding of where you are and what it will take to change.

The Word tells us: "The fear of the LORD is the beginning of wisdom; all who follow his precepts have good understanding" (Psalm 111:10).

# R — Repent

When you repent of any sin — including negativity — you simply do three things:

1. Ask God to forgive you.
2. Ask those you have harmed to forgive you.
3. Forgive yourself.

The Apostle Paul declared before King Agrippa, "I preached that they should repent and turn to God and prove their repentance by their deeds" (Acts 26:20).

# E — Exchange

The cure is complete when you exchange what you have been for what God expects you to be. You trade the problem for the solution — the impossible for the possible. In Christ you are a new creature. "Old things are passed away; behold, all things are become new" (2 Corinthians 5:17).

Jesus asked, "What good is it for a man to gain the whole world, yet forfeit his soul? Or what can a man give in exchange for his soul?" (Mark 8:36-37)

## Fifteen Vital Steps

If you are serious about defeating the critical, judgmental spirit Satan has targeted against you, here are fifteen specific things you can do:

**1. Learn to identify what is negative.**

The moment you are tempted to entertain a harmful thought or utter a harsh word — stop! Recognize what is taking place and keep your vow to fill the world with light instead of darkness.

As Paul advised, "Do everything without complaining or arguing" (Philippians 2:14).

**2. Be willing to change.**

Is transformation your idea, or the suggestion of someone else? The decision must be yours.

God declares: "If you really change your ways and your actions and deal with each other justly...then I will let you live in this place, in the land I gave your forefathers for ever and ever" (Jeremiah 7:5, 7).

**3. Seek Godly wisdom.**

Those who call themselves Christians should not be ruled by their feelings or give voice to anger or bitterness.

Instead, God is looking for men and women who live by strong principles and are guided by His knowledge and wisdom.

James wrote: "If any of you lacks wisdom, he should ask God, who gives generously to all without finding fault, and it will be given to him" (James 1:5).

**4. Surround yourself with positive, Godly people.**

One of the greatest powers you have been given is the power of choice.

Look around. Who are your friends and those with whom you spend a great deal of time? If they are not sources of inspiration and encouragement, it may be time to seek some new, positive Christian friends.

Listen to the words of Paul: "I appeal to you, brothers, in the name of our Lord Jesus Christ, that all of you agree with one another so that there may be no divisions among you and that you may be perfectly united in mind and thought" (1 Corinthians 1:10).

**5. Think positively.**

Do you need a guideline for an affirmative thought life? Here's a verse worth committing to memory: "Whatsoever things are true, whatsoever things are honest, whatsoever things are just, whatsoever things are pure, whatsoever things are lovely, whatsoever things are of good report;

if there be any virtue, and if there be any praise, think on these things" (Philippians 4:8 KJV).

## 6. Speak positively.

I was recently asked, "Keith, do you believe someone can be saved and ungodly at the same time?"

"Yes," I answered. It happens because of a tongue that has not been tamed, and a mind that does not stay spiritually focused.

Paul wrote to Timothy, "Set an example for the believers in speech, in life, in love, in faith and in purity" (1 Timothy 4:12).

## 7. Act positively.

Your belief is reflected by your behavior.

Since the world sees only our actions and not our thoughts, on a scale of one to ten, how are you communicating your faith?

Jesus said, "By this all men will know that you are my disciples, if you love one another" (John 13:35).

## 8. Refuse to judge others.

Some people don't wait to be elected to the position of a justice or magistrate — they appoint themselves.

If you want an instant cure for tension and seek peace and tranquility for your life, start loving instead of condemning. If God doesn't judge someone before they die, neither should we.

Scripture clearly warns: "Why do you judge your brother? Or why do you look down on your brother? For we will all stand before God's judgment seat" (Romans 14:10).

**9. Refuse to listen to negative people.**

Input determines output. If you give an ear to Satan, or those he inspires, you will soon be filled with what is evil and corrupt and it will taint your conversation.

The Bible says that he who does not heed the sound instruction of Christ "understands nothing. He has an unhealthy interest in controversies and quarrels about words that result in envy, strife, malicious talk, evil suspicions and constant friction between men of corrupt mind, who have been robbed of the truth" (1 Timothy 6:4-5).

**10. Believe the best in yourself and others.**

I'm sure you have heard the phrase, "The best is yet to come!" Do you truly believe it? Is it the basis of the decisions you make for yourself and how you judge the intentions of your associates?

Listen to the advice of Peter: "Show proper respect to everyone: Love the brotherhood of believers, fear God, honor the king" (1 Peter 2:17).

**11. See the best in yourself and others.**

What you look for you will surely find. Are you searching for things to criticize and condemn? Or are you looking for something worthy of your appreciation and applause?

The Lord says, "Whoever loves his brother lives in the light, and there is nothing in him to make him stumble" (1 John 2:10).

**12. Do your best for yourself and others.**

American business and industry could not survive the competition of a world marketplace without a commitment to quality. Is that also your objective? As someone who serves the King of Kings, is it your goal to reach your highest potential for the Lord?

Remember, God does not want us to be self-centered. "Each of you should look not only to your own interests, but also to the interests of others" (Philippians 2:4)

**13. Become a giver.**

Another way of saying "winning and losing" is this: "Giving and taking."

There are millions of people who journey through each day with only one objective — to see how much they can accumulate. God's rule of measure is not how much we have received, but what we have given. The Word tells us, "Each man should give what he has decided in his heart to give, not reluctantly or under compulsion, for God loves a cheerful giver" (2 Corinthians 9:7).

**14. Develop a grateful spirit.**

Have you adopted an attitude of gratitude? It's a perspective that pays more than earthly dividends; it is accompanied by the promise of God's blessing.

No matter if the water is smooth or the seas are rough, "Give thanks in all circumstances, for this is God's will for you in Christ Jesus" (1 Thessalonians 5:18).

**15. Ask the Holy Spirit to help you.**

I am thankful every day that when Christ ascended into heaven He did not leave us comfort-less.

The Lord said, "But the Counselor, the Holy Spirit, whom the Father will send in my name, will teach you all things and will remind you of everything I have said to you" (John 14:26).

That promise was fulfilled. The Holy Spirit is here now to be your teacher and guide. He is waiting for your call.

## It's Your Decision

Life is a series of choices, and by making the right decisions you will avoid aligning yourself with the devil.

God has shown you the way, yet He has placed you in charge. You are the author of the book of your life — the captain of your ship.

You are the one who allows harmful, critical thoughts to touch down on the landing strip of your mind. It is your heart that is the control tower and has the power to say, "That is a negative thought. I'm going to wave that one on by! That is a negative word. I'm not going to allow it to touch down on my life."

*You are writing a gospel, a chapter each day.*
*By deeds that you do and words that you say.*
*Men read what you write, whether faithless or true.*
*Say, what is the gospel according to you?* [2]

Will you take the message of this book and apply it today? Don't be like the children of Israel who wandered aimlessly for forty years because of a critical spirit and disobedience.

My prayer for you is that you will allow the Holy Spirit to cause you to be a positive, radiant light in a dark, troubled world.

*I pray God will give you a spirit*
*of revelation and wisdom.*

*I pray the Lord will depart*
*knowledge and understanding.*

*I pray that you will speak blessing
over others and declare God's
purpose and plan for your life.*

*I pray that the Father will give you
divine favor with man and that whatever
you set your hand to do will prosper.*

*And I pray that God will give you
the power to defeat Satan's number
one weapon — negativity.*

# Endnotes

1  Carlo Collodi; 1883, The Adventures of Pinocchio
2  Paul Gilbert; The Gospel According to You

# OTHER BOOKS BY KEITH A. CRAFT

Within the pages of his motivational and inspirational self-help book, *Your Divine Fingerprint: The Force That Makes You Unstoppable*, are the tools to help you discover a unique fingerprint that you have been given. These tools will help you deploy your unique difference that your family needs, your marriage needs, your job needs, your faith needs—that the world needs. And when you embrace and live in that uniqueness, you celebrate the glory of God.

*Leadershipology 101: Quotes to Live By* are inspirational quotes to propel you in your leadership quest. Keith has put together his collection of leadership quotes and has included a "Keith Craft's Thought Behind the Quote" to provide an additional thought to both challenge and inspire. *Leadershipology 101: Quotes to Live By* is an excellent resource of short, life-changing quotes which have given life to people worldwide.

A hero is someone who is admired for courage, achievements, or noble qualities. This perfectly describes how Allen sees his Mamaw. Through the inspiring life and words of Allen's grandma, his very first leadership life coach, you will be shown tenets that will change your life for the better. *Mamaw's Tenets for Life* is a leadership fable that introduces you to a different way of thinking and living that will empower you to be the best YOU, you can be.

Made in the USA
Coppell, TX
13 January 2022

71574661R00056